# God's Grace, Not My Disgrace

## Claudia Inglis

Olympus Story House

# CONTENTS

God's Grace, Not My Disgrace

Statement: Despite shame, God can overlook one's disgrace and cover the person with His healing forgiveness and grace.

### God's Grace, Not My Disgrace

*Amazing grace shall always be my song of praise,*
*For it was grace that bought my liberty;*
*I do not know just why he came to love me so,*
*He looked beyond my fault and saw my need,*
*I shall forever lift my eyes to Calvary,*
*To view the cross where Jesus died for me;*
*How marvelous the grace that caught my falling soul*
*He looked beyond my fault and saw my need.*

# Introduction

H e looked beyond my faults and saw my dire need. He became my loving Father, my comforter. He gave me assurance and was my sole consoler. He forgave me; most of all, He loves me." Amazing Grace shall always be mine. It was God's amazing grace that kept me, in light of my difficult situation that was causing the hurt and pain that affected my mind, body, soul, and spirit.

Assuredly it is the love of God who saved my soul by allowing His son, Jesus, to go through the crucifixion on the cross at Calvary to save my soul from eternal death and by Him coming down from the cross so I can live and be free from the bondage of sin. Through His grace, I became liberated from spiritual death by sin, especially through my shame and disappointments in life when I felt that I was not worthy.

I know He knew me from my mother's womb. I am His child; I was formed by Him with His earth, breath, and spittle. Unquestionably, that is why He loves me and because He loves me unconditionally, He covers me with His grace and mercy. By the blood and wounded stripes of His son, Jesus, I am healed. Consequently, that is why I will praise and worship Him daily as I look up to the place of Jesus' crucifixion, to attain and maintain that joy, praise and worship, that He has placed in my heart through His amazing grace.

# CHAPTER 1

# Inspiration Through Perseverance

I t feels amazing when I look back and see the plan the master had in store for me. I realized that He could only work through me, in me and around me; when I let go of the hurt and pain and release the handcuffs of destruction in my life to achieve spiritual maturity growth and fulfillment which is necessary for a blessed, abundant, productive and fulfilling life, and my requests can be accessed through my physical persistence and spiritual empowerment through perseverance, endurance, and prayer.

No one ever told me about the values I possess, what I could aspire to be or the potential I had of being a writer, poet, or a motivational speaker, which has always been my dream. I was never told that I had to pursue in depth writing, understanding the concept of the English language in diversified areas, the usage and application of words in writing and speaking, and how it would allow me to express myself when doing presentations, communications and letter writing.

As a child, I never had a television; I only had a radio, so I spent my time listening to music I loved from Dolly Parton, Jim Reeves, and Johnny Cash. I was always given books all the time as gifts which motivated me to read.

As I grew older, I got more interested in reading any paper or book in view on which I placed my hands. The only problem I had, and still have, is retaining what I had read to a certain extent. Reading enthuses and motivates me, as it is a form of using my mind and applying what I read or have read, and this is what has inspired me to continue to this present time.

I am a 70-year-old woman who has been through some mental, emotional, physical, and spiritual challenges. When I had a stroke in September 2001, I thought this would be the end for me, but it was the beginning of a prosperous journey when God inspired me to start writing. This started my healing process. I received the gift and ability to start writing in the early hours of the morning while I was being healed. I have been writing poems and messages and did not understand why I was doing all this writing, not realizing that someday, I will be publishing a book that was predestined by God.

My journey all started through a young lady I met; she saw in me what I did not see in myself. One day, she brought me an advertisement she had seen for counseling classes. As her daughter called me, she said to me, "Grandma, you need to go and call about this course because this is what you do all the time, you are always helping people out."

Unbeknown to her what my story was or to me what door was opening for me to walk through, but this was an opportunity to expand my place in God's kingdom. God used her to get me into the counseling class to help me first, so that I could reach out to others who went through the same afflictions as I did.

Romans 8:28 (NIV) says, "And we know that in all things God works for the good of those whose love Him, who has been called according to His purpose." I then put one foot forward and inquired about the class, addressed it and with God's help, I pursued it. Every Saturday for two years, I attended classes, which I successfully completed and graduated with a certificate in Christian counseling. After completion from this class, I did a ministry class for six months where I received a minister's certificate. I went to Suffolk Citizen Police Academy for one year where I graduated in the 25th class; I then joined the alumni association. I was then encouraged by one of my friends and mother in ministry to think about attending New York Theological Seminary Christian Program which I prayed about

2

and decided to attend for two years then graduated with a certificate in Christian Ministry.

Knowing that I have been writing with the intent to hopefully publish, it entered my mind to pursue Writing in Theology upon completion at the seminary. I thought this is an opportune moment and time to pursue this writing class, as it will empower me mentally and spiritually so I can get to the place God has destined for me and move in the purpose and plan He set before me. My high in life is to be able to put the writing through to reach the masses. God inspired me to put my experience in book format to help inspire, motivate, and encourage people to take them from a place of brokenness to wholeness, where healing is the ultimate purpose knowing in the end God will be glorified. My low in life is thinking: will this ever happen and when? I lived with this fear for years.

Then I remembered the scripture that Jesus said in Proverbs 3:5-6, "Trust in the Lord with all your heart; and lean not unto your own understanding. In all your ways acknowledge Him, and He will direct your path." I then began to reflect on these words, knowing that if I trust, believe, and have faith in God who brought me this far and stop trying to figure things out on my own and allow God to take over the reins, things can fall into prospective.

I have to recognize His existence through what I have been through and what I am able to do, acknowledging that He is the omniscient, omnipotent, omnipresent one who will never fail me but work things out on my behalf. I have to understand that God does not need me; I need Him for He will do what He said He will do if I only allow Him to do so on my behalf. Because of His unfailing love for me, He promised that He will never leave me or forsake me even in time of crisis, for this is the only greatest, unconditional love I can ever behold in my journey of life.

## CHAPTER 2

# My Greatest Love:
# My Enforcer

My greatest love and enforcer is my Lord and Savior Jesus Christ. He is loving, compassionate, and understanding. Certainly, I will start off by saying my greatest love in the earthly realm is my grandmother; she has been my enforcer in everything I did. Though she is deceased, the standard and principles she instilled in me still resides in me. The words "MY GREATEST LOVE" are very personal, sentimental, and significant to me in both the spiritual and worldly realm.

Looking at the word "my" (as only possession), "greatest" (very large in size, quantity, or number; powerful, influential, and of outstanding importance), "love" (deep affection and warm feeling for another, a strong person, a strong fondness or enthusiasm). This reflects my grandmother.

My grandmother, from what I understand, took me from my teen parents from the age of two years old to be of help to them since they were travelling back and forth. I was the firstborn, and my brother was one year younger than me.

My father was from the Caribbean islands, and my mother was from the Netherland Antilles where my father travelled and worked overseas. This was the place of residence for my parents at that time.

I remember as a little girl my grandmother hired someone to help her with chores in the home and also help care for me since I attended preschool at that time. She had to dress me, comb my hair, and take me to school; she always checked to assure I was well-groomed before we left the house.

My grandmother always made sure I read every day and relate to her what I read which made it interesting. She also assisted me with my homework, and by the age of ten, I was able to say my multiplication tables from two to twelve thoroughly. She was firm and disciplined with me, but she also allowed me free time with supervision. She was involved in my education and did so lovingly.

I remember having my own room, but my grandmother always came, prayed with me and tucked me in bed, then she would go to her room and pray. Since we were of Catholic faith at that time, she prayed the rosary every morning and night, said her novenas, and still went to church every day—morning and evening—while managing her own business. She always trusted leaving her employees while she went to church. God was number one in her life; everything else was secondary.

I can remember grandma taking me to church six days out of seven, which I always looked forward to and enjoyed immensely. She taught me my catechism, my confession prayer, the Holy Rosary, the Lord's Prayer, the Apostles' Creed. She taught me the purpose for praying, and looking back at the life she lived showed me the result of effective, fervent, and persistence prayer. She lived by the scripture in Joshua 24:15 (KJV), "But as for me and my house we will serve the Lord." As I look back, I see why she prospered; she left that impact on my life. She was always reading and praying with so doing, I was motivated to do the same.

While my grandmother raised me, she also took care of her mother, who was well-cared for as she did for me and also spent valuable time with her husband who also worked; we were all cared for efficiently. She gave me what I needed and not what I wanted. She was communicative and cooperative with her husband, caring and compassionate to me and her mother; she made sure we were properly clothed, well fed three nutritious meals a day, and were well-nurtured. Our clothes were always well-kempt, starched, and ironed, and the house was always meticulous; the person she hired helped her maintain this in the home.

Though she had her business, she never neglected either one of us; she had her husband who also required her attention because they worked together. She was committed and consistent in what she did; nothing was ever left undone or incomplete. She would not start doing anything if she could not complete and never did anything without asking for help.

Living with her was like being in a flower garden with beautiful roses. She did not realize that when she was not around, I was being stuck by the thorns, inflicting pain upon me, not being able to express how it was affecting me.

Grandma was committed to her prayer life; she had an altar set up in her room where I watched the flickering candles all the time. She prayed night and day. Every moment she had, I would hear her praying or singing. She was a woman with good character and integrity and had pride in what she did which had an imprint on our family and friends' lives.

Though grandma prayed, I do not know whether she was aware of my pain or did not know how to address the pain that was inflicted upon me through sexual molestation which started at the age of five. This started happening to me when the caretaker left me with a family friend whom I called uncle.

He would place me on his lap to read to me, and that's where I was fondled and at the same time being told it was alright. I know it was uncomfortable but did not know how to express this to anyone. This kept on happening; it was traumatic to me. After that experience, I was fearful of staying alone with any male.

As I grew older, at the age of 8 years old, I was able to go to my friend's a few houses away which was my safe haven. I usually took math lessons on Saturdays. This one day, when I was 9 years old, instead of going to lessons, I went to my friend's house and when I got home, my uncle beat me with a leather belt which gave me welts all over my body, then he sent me to the shower.

This made me angry, but I could not react disorderly because I was always taught to respect my elders. Leviticus 19:32 says, "Stand up in the presence of the elderly and show respect for the aged. Fear your God I the Lord." All I could do was cry. As I can reflect, this was a punishment for disobedience which I needed but I felt that was undeserving because I was not a disrespectful child and should have had a less aggressive punishment.

In this life, we go through the same if we are disobedient to God and His commands. When we disrespect our obligation to Him, we face punishment through the things we experience that's detrimental to us and our family.

How and when do you differentiate different levels of pain, hurt, and anger and not being able to speak up and express yourself? When you are told to keep quiet and don't answer or say a word for you are then told you are disrespectful? As you will see or recognize, this is what was expected from you as a child. The first pain was from my abuser, and the second pain was by me being disciplined even in my hurt. My reaction of disobedience was from my first pain which was wrong, but I was trying to justify my actions by my reaction at the wrong time, and in the midst of this, I was a victim of abuse not being able to express myself.

Have you ever felt helpless or hopeless and alone? You put on a smiling face, groom your hair, and dress well. Everyone sees your outer beauty, but they don't see your inner pain. That's just how I felt. But I must let you know you should not feel that way. God sees it all; His son, Jesus, is always with you. As my spiritual sister Sylvia always says, "His footprints are your footsteps." I had to remember that in Deuteronomy3:6. He said in His word, "Be strong and courageous. Do not be afraid or terrified because of them, for the Lord our God goes with you; He will never leave you or forsake you." Have you ever felt afraid and unsure of what to do? Proverb 3:5-7 states, "Trust in the Lord with all your heart, and lean not unto your own understanding but in all your way acknowledges Him, and He shall direct your path." Call on the name of "JESUS." He hears your voice. He is always listening. He just wants you to talk with Him. He said let your requests be made known unto Him. He is BIG DADDY.

He is our FATHER. He said to wait patiently, and He will give you the desires of your heart. Be still and know that He is God, one who forgives. Do not ever feel that God is too far away to help you even though it sometimes feels like your world is collapsing. Uneventful things tend to happen to us at times, and we try to resolve it on our own, but we are unable to get a way to get out of the situation right away. There is no friend that can help you in a predicament; we can't do anything without the help of God our Father.

Just remember that in the midst of calamity, God is always near; we just have to recognize then we will be able to feel His presence. Psalm 23 tells us, "The Lord is our Shepherd; He restores our soul; even in the valley of hurt and pain His rod and His staff will give us comfort."

We must always try to remember that when we think we are alone, God is with us; He sees our hurt and feel our pain even when no one else does. So don't ever give up. Keep looking to God to get the help that you need. God promises to be with us always. I had to do just that so I could be able to move on. Joshua 1:9 (NIV) says, "Be strong and courageous. Do not be terrified; do not be discouraged, for the Lord your God will be with you wherever you go." This scripture is enough to let us know no matter what has been inflicted upon us or any issue that has affected us cannot deter or overtake us. In the midst of my hurt, I had to remember these words.

After this pain of punishment by my uncle, grandma started sending me to the house of an elderly neighbor after school. There, I felt safe and happy.

I carried hatred, which is a word I detest, for my uncle for a very long time, because I felt that he should realize that I was hurting even if my grandma at that time, I assumed, didn't know or see my pain, or maybe she was masking it. As we know especially in those days for family credibility, everyone had to keep things quiet even though they were aware as they say to avoid shame and disgrace in the family.

Despite of all what I went through, I had grandma's principle of prayer. As I lay me down to sleep, I think of the song "Jesus loves me, this I know." I realize that God has always been with me and had placed angels in my life to guard me.

My greatest love, who is my grandma, had reflected the attributes of Jesus in her life through her caring, love, compassion, and understanding. She was always giving, sharing, and helping, teaching manners, respect, etiquette, and prayers. She always stressed commitment which meant do not start what you cannot finish, and always ask God for direction before you address it. She said don't be afraid to ask for help in anything you do. Grandma is my angel whom I will always cherish for the principles and standards she taught and the impact of her prayer life she left with me. This is what I reflect back in anything that I do. Sometimes we take things for granted and don't realize the value of what we have, whether person or thing, till we lose him, her or it.

> *My greatest love I have to hold*
> *Grandma's story that cannot be left untold*
> *The life she lived the love she gave*
> *Her Christian ways she did unfold*

No doubt a great love is one that is affectionate, compassionate, understanding and influential. Grandma not only instilled in me the love she had, but a love that's even greater—that love is the love of Jesus Christ and the love for Jesus Christ. Grandma's story will never be left untold for she was my angel and in me, her story lies forever in my heart.

# CHAPTER 3

# My Guardian Angel: My Lighthouse

A guardian angel, from what I believe, is someone who is kind, helpful, and will come to you at the opportune time. An angel, who takes special care of a particular individual, says words of encouragement to empower or warn us and will arrive or be present in a moment of crisis.

A lighthouse is a structure with a powerful light that gives a continuous or intermittent signal to navigators; or a beacon. It is so assuring to look back and see how one can impact the life of others in what we say and do and the energy that we can release to help one come through. The plan God has infused in us, the purpose He has placed in us to be used as His lighthouse to help empower people, especially those who are hurting, to direct them to a place of restoration, recognizing that God is the one doing the work.

We often tend to procrastinate and try to strategize things that are beyond our understanding. In such cases, all we do is make things worse, when we should have prayed about the situation and ask God to give us direction.

While I was going through a crisis and not being able to express my predicament and not finding the right person to whom I could relate was very troubling to me. Looking back over the years through my second phase of hurt and pain from the age of 12 years old through 18 years old, with the sexual abuse and incest from family and friends who should have been protecting me, was hurting me. I went through; not knowing where to turn and who to turn to had me in a perplexed state.

At the age of 18, it was then everything took a turn. I was being given extra attention so I would be willing to participate in a carnival pageant to replace someone who had withdrawn, which I did consent to and won second runner-up. I was expected to travel to another festival where there would be tourist attractions. As the costume I wore depicted the universe queen, depicting the sun moon and stars, everyone was mesmerized by the creativity of the costume so it became one of the main attractions. It caught the eyes of and drew the attention of the tourists who were visiting at the time.

It was Thursday afternoon, two days before this great finale. I did not feel any way excited or motivated; I was in no way looking forward to this occasion. My mind started wandering; I started having flashbacks reflecting on what I had been experiencing for years. It was then I saw a big picture I felt that no one was concerned about me; they were blinded otherwise, they would have noticed the hurt and pain I was going through. They officially had me involved for what they could accomplish for popularity and fame. It is very disheartening when you feel that no one cares. I felt that I was put in a shed with a little window, and it was opened for light to shine only when someone desired my service. It was heartbreaking, and I felt lost.

It was a beautiful day. I spoke to everyone and was saying my cheerful goodbyes. They kept on asking me where was I going. I did not know either. I just knew I had enough, and I felt confused, lost, despondent, discouraged, distressed. I just wanted to take my life. I had no will to live anymore. I remember when I was alone at home, I took a bottle of pesticide and drank from it, attempting to commit suicide. I thought I would be gone as there was no one around to stop me. I thought this was the end to my pain.

When I opened my eyes, I saw a family friend of ours who came to visit hanging over me. I was in the hospital bed with tubes in my nose and arms; I had an oxygen mask. I felt more ashamed than I did from the pain of my abuse because everyone saw me as an irresponsible, immature youth, seeking attention because of my outward action. No one saw that I was going to lose my mind or myself from my inward pain that I would end up as a dysfunctional child with mental instability. All what I got was a scolding. I was being ignored rather than loved. No one ventured to inquire about why I did this horrible thing. Their concern was all about me making the family look bad in other people's eyes. Then, I landed in a worse dilemma because I still could not express myself. I know the family friend who found me unconscious was an angel sent by God to save me. He said to me that he had found me lying down on the floor, and I was not moving, so he called the ambulance and got me to the hospital. I realize that he helped save me in the moment of crisis when everyone else thought that I was irresponsible and disrespectful by acting erratic in my action. It was then I felt more than ever how they totally abandoned me. I felt that no one wanted to visit me for fear of embarrassment or shame from what I had done.

I recuperated and went home from the hospital, but I was still alone and lost. I realized that I had to make positive decisions for my life and ask God for forgiveness and that He gives me direction as to what I should do with my life. I had to realize that I have to forgive, be calm, and put aside anger and hatred for my sake, so negativity and bitterness did not get rooted in my life that would cause me destruction.

I thank God that despite of my situation, my spiritual life was not infected because the God I thought had abandoned me in all I went through never gave up on me. He covered me with His grace. I never got involved in drugs or alcohol and choice of wrong friends. Hebrews12:14- 15 says, "Look after each other so that none of you fail to receive the grace of God." Watch out that no poisonous root of bitterness grows up to trouble you, corrupting many. God did not put demands on us; He gave us the ability to have free choice. We have freewill to make choices to better ourselves in our situation or go to the bottom. But our goal should be to aim for higher. We cannot live our lives saying what our parents did, or did not do, for we have to live on our merits and aim for higher. One thing I do know is that my God has kept me, and He is a loving Father who embraces me. He is an understanding Father who acknowledges me, a caring Father who willingly directs me; He sacrificed His life for me, comforted me, gave me all I need by being at my side in the midst of discomfort and distress. He embraced me with His loving arms, showing how much He cares, nurturing me in my affliction and in the midst of confusion, keeping me in a safe haven away from harm and danger. He took my depression to joy, loving me when I felt I was not loved, looking over me when I was shunned, scorned, and abused. Jesus, I know, is my greatest love who I can call on 24/7 without reservation and get a response. His grace suffices me for I know that the angels in heaven are rejoicing because of the path I took.

I am prepared for the great mission set before me by God to help save souls for Christ on the highways and byways—from prostitution, sexual molestation and abuse in any form. Psalm 91:11 (NLT) says, "For He will order His angels to protect me wherever I go."

Undoubtedly from what I believe, the purpose of angels is to be encouraging, warming, comforting, assuring. They also guide and protect one in a moment of crisis. And in my situation, this is evident—by the empowerment that the Trinity the Holy Spirit has prepared me for the great mission that has been purposed for my life.

# CHAPTER 4

# Holy Spirit the Trinity: My Empowerment

The Holy Trinity, from what I understand, is the triune God that is the Father (God), the Son (Jesus), and the Holy Ghost (Holy Spirit). That has been a pivot in my life from my mother's womb and a forceful strength for me throughout the years of my trial and testing. Having been a past victim of abuse and molestation and having had a history of personal withdrawal and isolation tendencies, no one but the Trinity and the blood of the Son Jesus Christ could have helped me overcome that dilemma in my life.

After the death of my father, I was redeemed, realizing that God took away the one who should have protected me but allowed the pain that was inflicting pain upon me. Then no sooner, my mom, who was diagnosed with hypertension and a medical condition relating to her heart, had to take excess medication. She was diagnosed with kidney failure, causing her to go for dialysis. In the interim she developed an ulcer on her foot which became infected, since she was not treated properly by the doctors, causing her to have below-knee amputation to her right leg. She gave up, and it was then she became unresponsive and flaccid. She was then attached to a respirator for life support. I knew then that that was leading to the end of her journey here on earth because prior to surgery, she had expressed that she was tired and that she was praying for God to take her. I was on my way to visit her at the hospital when a speeding car swerved and knocked off the bumper of my car. I and the passengers were not hurt. I came out and with the help of my friends tied the bumper in the trunk and continued to the hospital. I knew then, it was the merciful God who kept my friends and I safe, allowing me to accomplish what I had set out to do which was to visit my unresponsive mom, laying up in the hospital. Unbeknown to me, that was going to be my last visit with her.

When I arrived at the hospital and saw my mother lying there, I asked God to give me the courage to forgive my mother for my past hurts. I had been blaming her for what I went through as a child, and our communication was poor. At that moment, all I wanted was to be able to comfort and embrace her before she took her last breath. My friends and I began singing, praying and praising God; I then took her hand, and I remembered the words on Exodus 20:12 (NLT), "Honor your father and mother. Then you will live a long full life in the land the Lord your God is giving you." I also remembered the words Jesus spoke, that if you only believe, by His stripes and the blood of the lamb, you are healed. It was then I felt the Holy Spirit, and I started speaking to her, saying, "Mom, let everything go. I love you."

I felt a release and relief for me and her for I knew I felt deep down in my heart that she was ready to go to her Maker. I kissed her goodbye and went home at about midnight. The following morning, on awakening at 9:30 a.m., I prayed and then called my brother who reluctantly responded, not wanting to be the one to disclose to me any information about my mother's passing. I already felt and knew that my mom had gone home to be with the Lord, her Father, Maker and Redeemer.

After my mom's death, I became a woman with boldness, a new creature, speaking the words of Christ with authority, not holding back how I felt, walking the right path, and making the right decisions, knowing that God is present in all I do and wherever I go.

He is the fervent, vibrant, omniscient, omnipresent, omnipotent, Triune God who has been with me from my mother's womb and will be with me till the end. As I reflected over the years I was with my mother, I understood and realized that many words she spoke in my life were not to harm me, even though things did occur, which she had no control over. I got hurt in the interim which affected my mental and social well-being.

God used her as a spiritual guardian to guide and warn me. That is why I know that Jesus is the center of my joy. He gave me a mother and father, but He fathered me. I looked up to others for guidance and respect but was betrayed by false love and brought to a place where love was portrayed in the form of incest and self-gratification. It was the devil's way of saying, "I got you, innocent little girl." I was left to wonder why. Is love so painful? No, it is not for Jesus said in Hebrews 13:5 (NLT), "Never will I leave you or forsake you." The empowerment of God the Holy Spirit and the Trinity is indescribable; if I live the incredible, I will be able to do the impossible because of Jesus Christ who walks beside me. I had to understand that I do not belong to myself but to God my Father for when I say the "Our Father" I have to make it personal and connect with Him intimately on that level as a father-daughter relationship. Recognizing the power of His Son, Jesus Christ, and the sacrifices He made opened my eyes to a new light where I can look to Him as my fortress.

CHAPTER 5

# Jesus Christ: My Fortress

When I think about Jesus and all that He has done for me, I shiver, shout and jump, knowing that there is someone who cared enough for me, to trade His life as a sacrificial offering to atone for the sins of me and my family, His unconditional love, His obedience to His father by humbly complying with his requests, already knowing the suffering and pain He would have to go through so that I could be free and not enslaved spiritually. Why should I let the world dictate my future when they did not know what I went through the hurt and pain of misuse and abuse?

Jesus, the Son of God, left home at the age of 13 and then started teaching. At the age of 33, He died, allowing himself to carry a cross and be nailed to it after He was betrayed by one of His own. When trouble came, He was left alone. Everyone disowned Him. His mother was powerless for all this was preordained, and it was a commission that had to be accomplished. He was ridiculed, beaten, spat upon, and defeated. He was doing the will of His father. He died on the cross. He atoned for my sins, and He was the only righteous one prosecuted. He suffered and bore it humbly— the crown of thorns on His head, the nails in His hands and feet. They pierced His side, and He was stripped of His robe, which was sold. All this humiliation He went through for the world and me.

Recognizing and acknowledging what Jesus went through makes me wonder why I should complain, when I experience pain, physically, mentally, and emotionally.

My daughter is diagnosed with mental instability, and my son went through a rough patch. They both feel I put it on circumstantial evidence that their father was not around to be there for them. Now that their father is deceased and that they are grown, they have attained a level of responsibility and understanding as they view things differently, which relieves me of the burden they were carrying. It makes me question why anyone should turn to drugs and alcohol to mask what they are going through and develop a bigger problem which is addiction and lose their dignity, integrity, and identity not only in themselves but also in Christ Jesus. We have to love ourselves before we can love God whom we cannot see. Our Father in heaven is the one whom we can rely on in any given situation. Where and when do we come to the understanding that in the midst of our struggles, there is someone the Father in heaven gave us who is greater, who we can call on, trust, and rely on, and His name is "Jesus." Psam91:2 (NIV) says, "I will say of the Lord, 'He is my refuge and my fortress, my God, in whom I trust.'" We will recognize that life is a covering hovering over us, with intent that we keep secure and safe, but then when we divulge into wrongdoing and wrong thinking, our actions become demeaning.

We allow ourselves to get captivated by all the intricacies and complications of the world that life throws at us through the turmoil and torment that hound us and compresses us mentally and physically.

I know my Jesus; He lives in me and gives me the peace that passes all understanding. I love Him for who He is, for being true to His word, and for sacrificing His life for me so that I can have eternal life. Psalm 59:9-10 (NIV) "O my strength, I watch for you; you, O God, are my fortress, my loving God." What I have been through and what I'm going through cannot be compared to the sacrificial burden He bore for me.

The issues I experienced strengthened, fortified, and empowered me for each ladder I climb on this Christian journey. I won't look down at my problems for if I do, I will go down to the bottom and falter. Every issue is a broken rung, so I have to look up and move up to the next rung. Knowing that every time I do so I am moving up to my place of victory, I have to keep my eyes focused on the mountain top where I can get to the place so I can be victorious. I had to come to the understanding that I am no more a victim but a victor. I am no more condemned in a sinful broken state but travailed to a pinnacle of restored wholeness.

I have to remember that Jesus is always the center of my joy. He is the comforter, sustainer, and provider. His longsuffering was so I can be victorious over the demonic spirits that will cause me to sin and lead me to a place of brokenness.

We become fearful about what's the next thing in life that's about to happen; we tend to keep our minds so absorbed in the sad and destructive issues and negativity of life that will destroy our integrity. Why do we allow ourselves to fall into that dismal area? Where there is FEAR, which is false evidence appearing real, afflicting our minds, it leads us to a place of self-destruction. When in this situation, the best thing to do is to ask God to redirect our minds so we can spend time in positive thinking.

We should place our focus on the God-given power that is within us to find and release our own freedom from the pain and anguish of life and stir up the spiritual aspect of healing that is within us for a clear mind, pure soul, and productive and effective being in this life.

Despite of what we've been through, character, integrity, and good principles can lead us to a place where we will be looked at for who we are; not by our outward appearance or what we've been through but be recognized for whose we are by our inner spiritual wealth and being that illuminates through us from the inside out.

For healing comes from within out, not from out in. Matthew 5:14-17 (KJV), "Let your light so shine before men, that they may see your good works, and glorify your Father which is in heaven."

We have to come to the premise knowing whom we represent on this earth—ourselves, our children, our family, and our savior Jesus

Christ in this universe as a positive being, on a spiritual path of our Maker, Savior, and Redeemer who suffered for us and allowed His life to be taken as ransom so we can be free. Isaiah 53:5 (NIV) says, "The Messiah was pierced for our transgressions, He was crushed for our iniquities; the punishment that brought us peace was upon Him, and by His wounds we are healed."

Assuredly, the suffering He endured and the blood that was shed through His crucifixion on the cross has liberated us from the consequences of sin.

# CHAPTER 6

# Sin and Deliverance: Crisis Intervention

God has saved and redeemed me by giving of His only son, Jesus. He showed His humbleness through the crucifixion on the cross and was then placed in the tomb where He arose after three days. Now, He lives so I can be redeemed and have fullness of life spiritually. I also understand that salvation is deliverance from the power and effects of sin. It is also a way which God delivered me from eternal punishment, by erasing my sins from the legal document which is the Lamb's Book of Life and inputting the perfection of Jesus Christ.

I know I was saved when I gave my life to Christ which did take time; it was a process. I confessed with my mouth and believed in my heart that Jesus Christ was my Lord and Savior. That was in September 1997. I was then 45 years old. I felt a release from the things I used to do which included being promiscuous and excessive partying and drinking. It was not an overnight redemption, but I know I had to stop without delay, because I made a commitment to God who had a mandate on my life. I made the decision by choosing to be obedient, dependable, reliable, and to faithfully and truthfully walk this Christian Journey.

Although I had been going to church since I was a child with my grandmother and the standards were instilled in me, as I grew older,

I felt that I went to church so as to comply with rules of the home and as a form of respect, but in the interim, I also enjoyed doing it and had no resentments. It is a memory that I will always live with.

However, standing on my own faith, I had to abide by God's covenant as the Bible implies by applying and projecting it, so things can be manifested in a positive way in my life.

I was never a smoker and never used drugs. I did drink socially and partied every other weekend. When I did these things no more, I had disassociated myself from those friends that indulged. I was a lover seeking to be loved by someone but instead ended in wrong relationships which affected my life. When I look back at what hurt me in the midst of humanistic love and reflect on how Jesus carried His cross—the cross of our burdens and transgressions, our sinful ways and attitudes—my pain was nothing compared to that. Yes, it was painful and traumatic, but He carried them; the weight was unbearable, but He did not deny me despite my downfalls, when everyone else did.

I had to come to the understanding that he travailed by carrying this heavy wooden cross, fell multiple times under that burden, whipped and bruised, and nailed to that same cross with the crown of thorns on his head to save me through His unfailing love, grace, and mercy; He went through the pain, anguish and suffering so I can be free. Sometimes I ask, "Why me?" But knowing that He carried my burden and loves me for who I am, His child who He knew from my mother's womb, then I had to come to remembrance that Jesus never said a mumbling word on the cross. Luke 23:24 (NIV), "He said 'Father, forgive them, for they do not know what they are doing.' It included me in my sinful nature. John 10:10 (NKJV), "The thief does not come except to steal, and to kill, and to destroy. I have come that they may have life, and that they may have it more abundantly." He gave up His life not for me to destroy mine but to enjoy it to the fullest and best potential that He has given me.

Then I know I found a real love who will never use and abuse me, never harass me, never afflict or inflict wounds on me. His name is JESUS, the love of my life. He comforts, embraces, and lifts me up. He is my healer, my rock, and my beacon. He is my all in all that sustains me daily and gives me the strength, will, faith, and purpose to go on, knowing I had to get up each morning to go to work and deal with other people's life situations mentally and physically.

I had buckled up in me anger, animosity, hatred, fear, and resentment. It was trapped in my heart and mind against those who hurt me, the foul thoughts and anguish that deterred me from the things I wanted to do in my life. I was delivered from those sins. I focused on reading the gospel and the truthful messages it was delivering to me in my daily life so that I could have a better relationship with my Father God. As I reminisce over the past issues and pain that were inflicted upon me, I can use that as a tool for bettering myself, by helping a brother, a sister—man or woman—to walk through this journey, letting them know that tough times don't last always, but it is only a temporary state of insanity that will eventually turn around through prayer praise and worship for the betterment of life.

It made me understand that my brokenness that was mended and restored needed to be used for spiritual growth and ministry and not beating myself over the head despite what others thought of me, knowing that I became a new person in Christ Jesus. I had a new identity not as an abused victim but as a victorious woman by not turning to alcohol and drugs as others did for they are only temporary reliefs that will destroy you in the end and make you lose your level of awareness. My mind was transformed. I received a renewed spirit and recognized how I should live. I desired to be productive, successful, and evangelize to the world about the unfailing love of Jesus Christ.

I had to ask God for discernment so my spiritual eyes can be opened to see the prey that is creeping upon me and pray that it kept away from me, for if it does try to attack, it will be demolished by the spiritual force God has given me access to. 1 John 4:4 (NLT) "But I belong to God, my dear people. I have already won a victory over those victors who tried to destroy me, because the Spirit who lives in me is greater than the spirit who lives in the world." He is my strength and help in time of distress. With this belief, I can share the necessity of having faith and the power it generates so I can have a free heart and mind to receive salvation and deliverance.

Clearly then I can understand through Jesus's sacrifice the spiritual freedom and transformed mind I attain. I can face life's daily challenge in the workplace.

CHAPTER 7

# The Workplace:
# Faith Challenge

I had to realize that the workplace was just as important in my daily life as my church and my home. The workplace challenged my Christian beliefs, as I had to understand that there were many different denominations. I had to be careful to comply with the Jewish customs as a caregiver and address the client's needs appropriately. This included spiritual and dietary needs—what should be eliminated at certain times, their silverware for certain food products, and even how their tray should be set. When someone expired, the body had to be left alone until the Rabbi came. I had to be careful and ask the residents whether I can pray with them before I did despite of their mental status. It was a challenge. I had to understand that in all walks of life, there are Christian challenges to be met. I learnt to respect each other as a people and stay within the guidelines requested so that I would not be of detriment to anyone.

I also had to deal with certain personalities from coworkers, supervisors, and the administration. That was a challenge on its own because I had to learn what to accept, ignore, and stay in the parameters that were expected from me at work.

Another situation that challenged my Christian beliefs was working on Sundays and having difficulty getting Sundays off for special church events, services, and holidays such as Easter and Christmas.

I am aware that there are some people who do not care, but I believe that a certain protocol should be maintained for people with certain religious beliefs. This was also a form of abuse because there were no boundaries or limitations regarding individuals; the primary concern was the benefit of the institution and their accomplishments. Primarily in this era, we have lots of family issues, and they revolve around work. I will go to work, and then come home to sleep, go shopping, talk on the phone, fix dinner, and will start a conversation which ends up revolving about work. We discuss what goes on there—how we are underestimated, how we have negative and noncompliant employees, their mannerisms and work ethics. This can draw our attention away from the family where we need to be focused. That may be the reason why we rarely have adequate Christian ethics instilled in our family. We take our focus off the family, and this causes a breakdown in communication and commitment. We need a Christian structure along with proper communication.

A workplace is not pleasant and happy without the spiritual joyful atmosphere. These standards have to be met despite what is going on or what you've been through. I feel that one has to be free to evangelize without restrictions in order to maintain a Christian foundation in any arena. Especially when you have been transformed from your brokenness, you want to let the world know of the greatness and glory of Jesus.

Besides the daily challenges in the workplace, there is nothing comparable to daily family problems. However, Christian belief is foundational.

# CHAPTER 8

# Family Impact:
# On my Christian Beliefs

L ooking back over my life and wondering how I made it, I reflect on the upbringing and teaching of my grandmother. I know there are some Christian beliefs and standards she left imbedded in me.

My early beliefs relating to Christians were that they should be very quiet people—seen and not heard. They should have a prayer life, pray in the quietness of their home or at church, should pray at all times, should not hang around the street corners socializing, should wear long dresses, and bodies should not be exposed. They should be kind, caring, serving, giving, comforting, supportive, loving, honest, and respectful.

As I grew older, I started looking at Christianity from a different perspective, realizing it is not only the outward appearance but also the inward being. We tend to uplift and hold high the people of our family with regards to ethnicity, skin color, grade of hair, financial status, the house they live in, level of education they attained, and school or college they attend or attended. Yet those who are poor and less fortunate, who have issues that would delay their level of opportunity or success, would be frowned upon.

I am one who can identify with these situations. We fail to realize that God is in the midst of each and every one in our lives, and He loves us despite of who or what we look like. He looks upon the lowly as much as He would with those who are self-righteous. We have to come to a place where we can become unified knowing that through it all, despite our indifferences from our hurt and pain, it should not separate us but strengthen us. We are individuals who should not be individualized, for we are one bloodline, one family serving one God who knows each downfall and accomplishment. God has purposed us for betterment. So we have to acknowledge this and glorify God in every situation, knowing that He did not suffer on the cross to save us from sin so love can prevail, for us to fail Him, for He lives so we can live likewise. We must embrace forgiveness and gratitude for each other knowing that one's family is very important in their life. Family is a pillar by which we are held up, fortified, and edified. Family is also our compass as a pathway in life, giving directions and information. They also become a source of force. This is what my grandma was to me.

All in all, God is the ultimate force in our lives. When we know God's desire for us and most importantly know our desire in Him and for us to feel His presence, we can be secure and bask in His grace, knowing that He is our pinnacle.

Although there were many obstacles, inflictions, and afflictions that tried to hinder and deter me through my teen years—the sexual and mental abuse, rejection, dealing with how I felt that I was an unwanted child which led me to attempt suicide—I still had to be there for my siblings even after my recovery. I had to help maintain a house and help prepare their meals and still go to school. I remember that I did it all with love, a smiling face, and a cheerful heart in the midst of all my pain. I can never remember being an angry child. I kept hoping that someday, someone would notice my hurt, pain, and the anguish that I was going through, but no one did. Through it all I received the strength, willingness, persistence, and perseverance to move on in my Christian walk. These beliefs were applied even though there were some changes which took place in my life that altered some of my beliefs and had me in doubt at times.

Grandma always taught me to listen and by doing so I would be able to hear and understand what someone was saying. I would have the discernment to know whether something was right or wrong and to be able to apply what I heard effectively to my life. I was taught always to respect others, whether young or old, rich man or beggar, drunk or sober, saved or unsaved, addict or not, no matter what status, for to earn respect, you have to give it. In sharing, if someone asked for something, never hold back no matter what little you have; always be willing to share knowing that the Lord will make a way somehow.

In giving, do not deny someone anything that is asked of you. Even though it's something you cherish, it should be extended to others. Always be willing to serve in the church, on the job, or share with a needy person.

I have come to realize that in praying, I must be reverent but not silent. The world should know that you are a praying person. You can pray openly for anyone and anywhere. We must sincerely and honestly share the gospel without any reservation and be supportive to people with their shortcomings. We must be confident in what we do, joyful with the expectation that something good is going to eventually happen, and most of all, we must love, for love supersedes all despite our circumstance or situation.

I will be strong and courageous as I go forward. I have full confidence that God will make me victorious in the end, so that I will be able to go through difficulties and hindrances with firmness and without fear. I declare that I am bold and brave, that I will fulfill my calling in the spirit of determination and overcome any obstacle that may be placed in my path. I will always be persistent in what I have to do and persevere until I can attain what is needed to achieve my Christian purpose successfully and effectively. This brings me to the place to understand that the Christian principles that were embedded in me from my grandmother's teaching now leads me to the church where I can impart what I have learnt to others. However, having embraced Christian belief and principles, I still need the church as a support system for my worship experience.

# CHAPTER 9

# Forgiveness: The Healing Source

I n the midst of my everyday activities, Sunday was my day of worship. One Sunday afternoon in 2005, when I came home from church and sat down on my couch on entering my home, I received the words "God's grace not my disgrace." I wrote the words down and never thought about it anymore. I never thought that I would be writing a book. I knew what I had experienced in my life from the age of 5 till the age of 18 but as time went by, I was then recognizing that God has great plans for me.

I realized that if I had not gone through the situation in my life, I would not have recognized the God-given ability in me to reproduce the seed that was placed in me from my mother's womb by God my Father.

We all have been broken and bruised at some point in our lives, in one way or another, but it is nothing compared to what Jesus went through. He did not cover up anything; He was authentic. When we are traumatized, we put something over the bruise to cover it up to take away the pain and discomfort, temporary relief that is prayer and scripture. But deep down in our hearts, there is the lingering pain of unforgiveness that remains, and it can affect our spiritual, physical, and mental medical well- being.

I know that grace is unmerited favor. It is also the power to overcome what you are going through. When everything became chaotic and everyone turned their back on me because of my downfall and I had no way out, I had to build up my strength through the word of God as this was the testing time of my faith, knowing that no one can help me but God. He is the only one who can bring me out of any situation. As I remember the poem "Footprints in the Sand"—whose author is unknown—for each situation in my life, there I saw two sets of footprints and realized God has been with me all along on this journey. But when I took my focus off, I only saw one set of footprints and got disheartened, and I had to get my grip and come to remembrance that God was always with me even in my moments of trials; he never left my side. In life, we have to know that God wants us to call out and reach out to Him and know that if I forgive and forgive those who have hurt me, I will receive healing. In His Word (Deuteronomy 31:6), "Be strong and courageous. Do not be afraid or terrified because of them, for the Lord your god goes with you; He will never leave you or forsake you."

In life, I have to get to that place of awareness that God is present and at our side always so that when I got to the place of discernment, I was able to feel His presence, hear his voice, and be able to reverence Him with forgiveness in my heart so I can be used by Him. With a purpose and determination to better myself by steering towards the positive leaving behind the negative. I had to regain what I had lost in the midst of this crisis, gain back my dignity, pride, and self-worth and in the process, remain humble, which led me to a place of worshipping in the church.

CHAPTER 10

# The Church:
# My Spiritual Impact

W hen we look at the word church, some of us refer to it as a building, where as it is an assembly of Christian believers who, existing under the discipline of the word of God, are organized to carry out that great commission, administer the ordinances, and manifest spiritual gifts ordained by Christ which leads to the church mission. When talking about the kingdom of God, we sometimes think of the following: to forgive, proclaim the word to the poor, pray for healing and deliverance, give service instead of receiving it, feed the hungry, clothe the naked, and provide for the needy both spiritually and physically.

We tend to clutch and focus on to denomination and not clarify our status or purpose of how effective we are in guiding the people in their spiritual walk and the healing we can bring about to those hurting and afflicted.

Jehovah God's mission for the church is to preach the gospel to the lost so they will come to obedient faith in Jesus Christ and be saved. Nurture and strengthen those who have already been saved. Do well to everyone especially to "the family of believers." Worship Jehovah God and Jesus Christ our Lord.

The church mandate is to serve Christ, the Head of the Church, in a manner made known to them through scripture, tradition, prayer, and experience.

They will demonstrate their commitment to this mission by their participation in worship and celebration; individually increasing our faith and understanding through prayer and study; caring one for the other as expressed in their fellowship together; continually broadening their outreach to needs beyond their particular community; faithfully speaking to the issues of the day; generously giving of their time, talents, and financial resources.

The mission statement of the church I attended is to increase our love for God and help meet the needs of human kind by "loving God with all our heart, with all our soul, and with our entire mind, and to love our neighbor as ourselves."

We also share in the mission of His Son, Jesus Christ, in "healing the sick, helping the blind to receive sight the lame to walk, the leper to be cleansed, the deaf to hear, the dead to be raised, and the poor to have the Good News preached to them" (Luke 4:18-2). We actualize this mission by praising God, being obedient to the demands of the gospel, telling the story of God's gracious acts in creating and redeeming the world, inviting persons to commit their lives to Jesus Christ, and serving as ministers of God's liberating and reconciling grace.

Every church should have a mission statement so that Christian ethics and standards can be met. Referring to other denominations and their mission statements there is a similarity, and there is a common thread, for all churches should be under one God-head, and their purpose should be the same to win souls for Christ.

The objective of Christian education is "to aid persons in the cultivation of the ability and disposition to acquire intelligently, and maintain effectively membership in the church of their choice."

The church is fulfilling its mission to the best of their ability as led and directed by the pastor.

My place in the church is effective to me in my Christian walk. I was consecrated a deaconess and appointed a class leader. These positions have helped me to be productive through spiritual teachings and guidance and as a support to the pastor to encourage membership in their Christian learning, spiritual uplifting, and growth.

Although there are many denominations, they all have one purpose, one mission, one goal to save the lost souls and get them to know the gracious, forgiving, merciful God through one church, one faith, one baptism.

The church I found out was where I continued to receive my spiritual foundation by reading and studying the word of God. Through this, it helped me maintain a family structure where I was able to identify my right and wrongdoing. By studying the word of God, it helped transform me and my family's lives to an atmosphere where love can abide, putting away the past and recognizing that our betterment and strength is built up through our downfalls.

I reflect and wonder sometimes if we were one church and one faith, because I noticed we are more segregated. Separated worshipping and idolizing the pastors happen. Pastors elevating those who are well-off financially or in their favor made me stay away from church for a while. I became introverted and withdrawn. I thought that I would go back to church and seek help. As the mothers of the church say "God will make a way." Then I saw things that were not pleasing. People's actions and reactions made me question if this is where I should be. I know I loved God but did not understand why I had mixed emotions. I stopped going to church at intervals questioning, "Am I doing what God wants from me?"

To the church I would encourage them to look at each person as a likeness of Jesus, do what Jesus would do which is to embrace and reassure comfort in the midst of what they are going through, recognizing that we all go through crisis, pain, and suffering. We all express it differently; some of us internalize, some in the way they dress or their actions but we, as Christians, ought to ask God to view people with our spiritual eyes in any given situation.

I observed that people will go to the altar over and over and not releasing their pain for fear of being judged by others or become the topic in church. We, as the church, talk about or neglect those who have been imprisoned, not realizing that we also are in prison in our everyday life when we walk around in pain from hurt and abuse, whether it be physical, spiritual, sexual, emotional, or drug abuse. It is prison if we are going through in pain secretly. No one knows but God knows.

Then we go to the altar for prayer repeatedly and yet your pain still goes unrecognized, that pain is the key to the prison in your life. From my youth to adulthood, I observed altar calls being done; people were falling out in the spirit. From what I observed, it was for a feel-good experience when it should be for miraculous healing. I say "feel good" because they would be talking about how they went out on the floor when the purpose of being slain is for miraculous healing and able to give a testimony to win souls to Christ. We have to come to a place where we become transparent and deny everyone for the only fear we should have is of God.

Jesus went to the cross where He experienced pain and suffering for our sake, but He triumphed over his crucifixion. So the same way, we need to praise God in our distress and pain knowing that we will overcome and move beyond and above the situations in our lives and be victorious in the end. The church has to realize and reflect that our Lord was not judgmental; He forgave us so we in turn should be able to see the good in each person and forgive each other. As Christians, we should reach out and help each other. Each one of us have to examine ourselves before we can cast judgment on anyone for we are all striving to reach perfection for only Jesus Christ is perfect.

As time went on, I left New York and traveled to Florida in search for a place of worship. I eventually got a Hispanic church where I felt accepted, and I was able to participate because it was bilingual. They also allowed me to participate and use my gifts and ministry which gave me the opportunity to do some of what I felt God had called me to and which allowed me to be bold in my walk for Christ. Then my pastor relocated, and I found another Hispanic church where I felt at home. It was family-oriented. There, I had no reservations because of the acceptance and brotherly and sisterly love. Principles and discipline are established there, but each one is able to participate in different areas of ministry all in the name of Lord our Savior. Jesus Christ is the forefront of this. This is a place where the pastors reach the heart and save the soul if you are willing to let God do the work. The church was established to fill the soul of men with the gospel and encouragement in the right way to be fruitful and spiritually endowed not the behavior of men

There is a song that I cherish by the title "He Looked beyond My Fault" (by Dottie Rambo, adapted from Londonderry Aires):

*Amazing grace shall always be my song of praise,*
*For it was grace that bought my liberty;*
*I do not know just why he came to love me so,*
*He looked beyond my fault and saw my need,*
Refrain: *I shall forever lift my eyes to Calvary,*
*To view the cross where Jesus died for me;*
*How marvelous the grace that caught my falling soul,*
*He looked beyond my fault and saw my need.*

# Conclusion

Assuredly, despite my downfall, my sinful life, and my hurt, my greatest love Jesus looked beyond my disgrace and covered me with His grace to allow me to take this Christian journey to serve Him faithfully, freely, and joyfully to fulfill the mission.

Admittedly, the greatest love grandma instilled in me through her story that stays in my heart is the love of Jesus; she was the angel who protected me in my childhood days. Her angelic spirit still guides me to this day, besides the empowerment of the Trinity and the Holy Spirit that prepares me for the great mission. Granted, through the sacrifice Jesus made, to allow His light to shine in my life by forgiveness and freedom from sin.

However, this has allowed me to endure daily workplace challenges, which help that have been filtered to me through the mission discipline and standards set by the church. Nevertheless, through it all, climbing the ladder of Christian faith and belief, I have one purpose and vision which is to win souls for Christ, teach the word to fulfill their soul, and accomplish that mission mandated by Christ.

# Appendix

As I write, I reflect and in my mind's eye view, I see how many of us have been abused, and the world is unaware of this happening every second, every minute, every hour in homes, schools, churches, and workplace. We need to have awareness concerning this epidemic. The parties involved should not just be imprisoned, but they should be counseled to a place where they can reconcile themselves to know God better and to have a personal relationship with Him. We have to realize hurt people hurt others because they never get the help they need. As the saying goes, "what would Jesus do (WWJD)."

Abuse is when someone takes privileges of their own to impose themselves upon another without consent. It can be horrific, terrifying, and petrifying. This can cause one to become rebellious, have fear, anger, rejection, and pain. Pain is felt as the hurt instilled upon you by another, be it a friend, parent, husband, wife, children, or siblings. This can lead to distorted thinking or decision-making causing drastic misunderstanding affecting family life and relationships.

Let us not be thrashers of another person's integrity or character. We in the world are not aware that most times, the one who hurt you in any form of abuse may have also been hurt and traumatized themselves but never got help. Some people are incarcerated when caught but where is justice instead of guidance and counseling to prevent the continuity of such pain amongst our people.

We have to realize this and not talk about the situation as a means of monetary gain when we address it but seek help for all parties involved. This is a silent pandemic that's been infiltrated in our lives, and we have to find a resolution. I know that having gone through this it is inexplicable because no one understands. They question, "Why did you not say something?" How you felt when told no one will believe you. Then you are traumatized and fearful so you remain in the place where you are manipulated and walk around like nothing is wrong when indeed you are broken, but for the grace of God.

As I went through this traumatizing experience of abuse, there was JESUS. I used this encounter as a means of developing my spiritual growth for in the midst of this, it is a learning experience to help others along the way. God kept me in a sound mind. I maintained my self- esteem through my character and integrity and encourage others to cross that threshold to the next step in their life.

Through sincere forgiveness, the victim will forgive themselves and forgive the abuser so that they both can be healed to be able to continue on the road of recovery to achievement and success.

When we withhold the things which has harmed us, we feel that we have no self-worth, that the world will judge us if we speak out. There should be no fear for God will not judge you; the world may close doors but God opens doors; the world may scorn you but God loves you; the world will curse you but God will anoint you.

Reflect on this scripture from Psalm 121:1-8: Look up to the hills from where comes your help it comes not from man but from the Lord. He will make you rise above your situation for when you look up, the higher you go; if we look down, the lower we fall. We deceive ourselves through denial and pretense to please those who are around us instead of being open and honest about the situation which will release that chain of bondage that tries to entrap us, leading us to a place of depression where we may turn to alcohol, drugs, and eventually suicide. Let not your heart be troubled; the world has nothing to offer you, but God has. He supplies all your needs. Stay strong, seek guidance, keep the faith. Call on someone when in crisis; everyone is not out to hurt you. Call on the name of JESUS. He will put someone in your path at the right time to pull you out of that messy pool or help you get to that next level to where you can increase in your God-gifted potential. It does not matter about the church despite all the pain and hurt you have endured. It matters about Me. Jesus Christ, the one and only who will be with you always for my grace abounds over every situation and circumstance. I will always be your greatest LOVE. For it is not about your disgrace, but it is about my GRACE.